AF865206

TECH WORDS FOR NORMAL HUMANS

A Plain English Guide to AI, Coding & App Design Terms

By

Beam Frankland

Understanding technology without the confusing jargon.

Copyright © 2026 by Beam frankland

All rights reserved.

No part of this publication may be reproduced, distributed, or transmitted in any form or by any means without prior written permission from the author, except in the case of brief quotations used in reviews.
This book is intended for educational purposes only. While every effort has been made to ensure accuracy, the author makes no guarantees regarding the completeness or suitability of the information provided.

ISBN: 978-1-7640123-0-0

DISCLAIMER

This book simplifies technical terminology related to AI, coding, and app development for educational purposes. It is not intended to replace professional software development training, legal advice, or technical consultation.

Technology evolves rapidly. Some tools, platforms, and practices described may change over time.

Readers are encouraged to seek professional guidance when building production-level applications or handling sensitive data.

The author is not responsible for outcomes resulting from the use of information in this book.

HOW TO USE THIS BOOK

This book is designed to make technical language easier to understand.

Each term follows the same structure:

What Developers Mean
A clear explanation of the technical definition.

Plain English
A simplified translation that makes the concept easy to understand.

Real-Life Example
Where you've likely seen this in everyday apps.

How to Say It to AI
A practical example of how to use the term when prompting AI or discussing with developers.

You do not need to read this book in order.

Use it as:

- A reference guide
- A confidence booster
- A translation tool when working with developers
- A companion when building apps with AI

If you ever think, "What does that mean?"
Flip to the term and decode it.

TABLE OF CONTENTS

Section 1 - UI & Screen Terms
Page 6
Button
Card
Carousel
Checkbox
Container
Dropdown
Footer
Grid
Header
Icon
List View
Modal
Navigation Bar
Placeholder
Pop-Up
Radio Button
Scroll View
Sidebar
Tab Bar
Text Field

Section 2 - How Apps Think
Page 27
Array
Boolean
Click Event
Conditional (If/Else)
Event
Fetch
Function
Loop
Object
On Submit
Parameter
Refresh
Render
State
Variable

Section 3 - Data & Systems
Page 43
API
Authentication
Backend
Cloud
Database
Domain
Endpoint
Frontend
Hosting
Server

Section 4 - Design & UX
Page 54
Accessibility
Alignment
Margin
Padding
Prototype
Responsive
Typography
UI (User Interface)
UX (User Experience)
Wireframe

Section 5 - Development Process
Page 65
Bug
Debug
Deployment
Framework
Git
Production
Repository
Testing
Update
Version

SECTION 1

UI & SCREEN TERMS

BUTTON

A clickable element that triggers an action..

What Developers Mean:

A UI component that responds to user interaction (click or tap) and executes a function.

Plain English:

A digital "press me" object.

Real-Life Example:

"Buy Now"
"Sign Up"
"Submit"

How to Say It to AI:

"Create a primary button styled in dark blue with rounded corners."

Personal Notes

CARD

A grouped content block that displays related information.

What Developers Mean:

A rectangular container used to organize content such as images, text, and actions.

Plain English:

A neat little information box.

Real-Life Example:

A product listing with image, title, and price.

How to Say It to AI:

"Design a product card with an image at the top and a button at the bottom."

Personal Notes

CAROUSEL

A swipeable content slider.

What Developers Mean:

A horizontally scrollable component used to display multiple pieces of content in the same space.

Plain English:

Slides you flick sideways.

Real-Life Example:

Featured products on a shopping app.

How to Say It to AI:

"Add a carousel at the top that auto-slides every 5 seconds."

Personal Notes

CHECKBOX

A small square that allows multiple selections.

What Developers Mean:

A form input that lets users select one or more options.

Plain English:

Tick the box.

Real-Life Example:

"I agree to the terms."

How to Say It to AI:

"Add a checkbox users must select before submitting the form."

Personal Notes

CONTAINER

A layout wrapper that holds other elements.

What Developers Mean:

A structural component used to group and style UI elements together.

Plain English:

An invisible organizing box.

Real-Life Example:

A section holding a heading and paragraph.

How to Say It to AI:

"Wrap this section in a container with 20px padding."

Personal Notes

DROPDOWN

A hidden list of options that appears when clicked.

What Developers Mean:

A collapsible selection component for choosing from a list.

Plain English:

Click to reveal choices.

Real-Life Example:

Country selector in a form.

How to Say It to AI:

"Create a dropdown with five selectable options."

Personal Notes

FOOTER

The bottom section of a screen or page.

What Developers Mean:

A persistent bottom layout area often containing links and legal information.

Plain English:

The closing section.

Real-Life Example:

Privacy Policy | Contact | Terms

How to Say It to AI:

"Add a simple footer with navigation links."

Personal Notes

GRID

A layout made of rows and columns.

What Developers Mean:

A two-dimensional system used to align and organize content.

Plain English:

Content arranged in neat boxes.

Real-Life Example:

Privacy Policy | Contact | Terms

How to Say It to AI:

"Display products in a 3-column grid."

Personal Notes

HEADER

The top section of a screen.

What Developers Mean:

The upper layout area containing title or navigation.

Plain English:

The page's introduction bar.

Real-Life Example:

Page title at the top of an app.

How to Say It to AI:

"Create a fixed header with the page title."

Personal Notes

ICON

A small visual symbol representing an action.

What Developers Mean:

A graphical element used to communicate meaning quickly.

Plain English:

A tiny picture that replaces words.

Real-Life Example:

Shopping cart symbol.

How to Say It to AI:

"Add a search icon to the top right."

Personal Notes

LIST VIEW

Items displayed vertically in a single column.

What Developers Mean:

A layout pattern for displaying structured data in rows.

Plain English:

One thing under another.

Real-Life Example:

Email inbox.

How to Say It to AI:

"Display messages in a list view."

Personal Notes

MODAL

A pop-up window that blocks interaction with the rest of the screen.

What Developers Mean:

An overlay component that requires user action before returning to the main interface.

Plain English:

A "pause everything" box.

Real-Life Example:

"Are you sure you want to delete?"

How to Say It to AI:

"Open a modal when the delete button is clicked."

Personal Notes

NAVIGATION BAR

A menu that helps users move around the app.

What Developers Mean:

A persistent navigation component placed at the top or bottom.

Plain English:

The app's map.

Real-Life Example:

Home | Search | Profile

How to Say It to AI:

"Add a bottom navigation bar with three tabs."

Personal Notes

PLACEHOLDER

Temporary text inside an input field.

What Developers Mean:

Instructional hint text that disappears once the user types.

Plain English:

Example text that vanishes.

Real-Life Example:

"Enter your email..."

How to Say It to AI:

"Add placeholder text inside the search field."

Personal Notes

POP-UP

A temporary floating message.

What Developers Mean:

A UI element that appears over content to display information or request action.

Plain English:

A surprise message window.

Real-Life Example:

“Subscribe to our newsletter.”

How to Say It to AI:

“Trigger a pop-up after 5 seconds.”

Personal Notes

RADIO BUTTON

A circular option where only one can be selected.

What Developers Mean:

A single-choice selection input control.

Plain English:

Pick one only.

Real-Life Example:

Small | Medium | Large

How to Say It to AI:

"Use radio buttons for selecting subscription type."

Personal Notes

SCROLL VIEW

A screen that moves when content doesn't fit.

What Developers Mean:

A container allowing vertical or horizontal scrolling.

Plain English:

Swipe to see more.

Real-Life Example:

Social media feed.

How to Say It to AI:

"Wrap this page in a scroll view."

Personal Notes

SIDEBAR

A vertical side menu panel.

What Developers Mean:

A collapsible navigation panel that appears from the side.

Plain English:

A hidden side drawer.

Real-Life Example:

Hamburger menu sliding out.

How to Say It to AI:

"Add a collapsible sidebar menu."

Personal Notes

TAB BAR

A row of clickable tabs inside a screen.

What Developers Mean:

A segmented control used to switch between views.

Plain English:

Digital folder tabs.

Real-Life Example:

Reviews | Details | Specifications

How to Say It to AI:

"Create a tab bar with two sections."

Personal Notes

TEXT FIELD

A box where users type information.

What Developers Mean:

An input control for capturing user text.

Plain English:

A typing box.

Real-Life Example:

Login username field.

How to Say It to AI:

"Add a required text field for full name."

Personal Notes

SECTION 2

HOW APPS THINK

ARRAY

A structured list of related items stored together.

What Developers Mean:

An ordered collection of values stored under a single variable name. Items inside an array are accessed using index positions.

Plain English:

A row of labeled boxes that hold similar things.

Real-Life Example:

A list of products in your cart.
A list of comments on a post.

How to Say It to AI:

"Store the product names in an array and display them in a list."

Personal Notes

BOOLEAN

A value that can only be true or false.

What Developers Mean:

A binary logical data type representing one of two possible values: true or false.

Plain English:

A yes-or-no answer.

Real-Life Example:

Is the user logged in? → True
Is dark mode enabled? → False

How to Say It to AI:

"Create a boolean that tracks whether the user is logged in."

Personal Notes

CLICK EVENT

An action triggered when something is clicked or tapped.

What Developers Mean:

An event listener that detects when a user interacts with a clickable element.

Plain English:

When someone presses something, something happens.

Real-Life Example:

Click "Add to Cart" → Item gets added.

How to Say It to AI:

"Trigger a click event when the button is pressed."

Personal Notes

CONDITIONAL (IF/ELSE)

Logic that makes decisions based on conditions.

What Developers Mean:

A control structure that executes different code depending on whether a condition evaluates to true or false.

Plain English:

If this happens → do this.
If not → do something else.

Real-Life Example:

If password is correct → log user in.
Else → show error message.

How to Say It to AI:

"Add an if/else condition that checks whether the user is logged in."

Personal Notes

EVENT

Something that happens in the app.

What Developers Mean:

A user-triggered or system-triggered action that the application can detect and respond to.

Plain English:

A moment that causes a reaction.

Real-Life Example:

Clicking a button.
Submitting a form.
Loading a page.

How to Say It to AI:

"Create an event that runs when the page loads."

Personal Notes

FETCH

To retrieve data from another source.

What Developers Mean:

A request made to an external resource (usually an API) to retrieve data.

Plain English:

Asking another system for information.

Real-Life Example:

Getting weather data.
Loading product listings.

How to Say It to AI:

"Fetch product data from the API when the page loads."

Personal Notes

FUNCTION

A reusable block of instructions that performs a task.

What Developers Mean:

A defined block of code that runs when called and may accept inputs and return outputs.

Plain English:

A small machine that does one job.

Real-Life Example:

A function that calculates total price.
A function that sends a confirmation email.

How to Say It to AI:

"Create a function that calculates the total cart price."

Personal Notes

LOOP

A way to repeat something multiple times.

What Developers Mean:

A control structure that executes a block of code repeatedly until a condition is met.

Plain English:

Do this again and again.

Real-Life Example:

Displaying every product in a list.
Showing each comment under a post.

How to Say It to AI:

"Use a loop to display all items in the array."

Personal Notes

OBJECT

A structured collection of related information.

What Developers Mean:

A data structure made up of key-value pairs representing properties and values.

Plain English:

A labeled folder with details inside.

Real-Life Example:

User object:
Name: Sarah
Email: sarah@email.com
Role: Admin

How to Say It to AI:

"Create an object that stores user profile details."

Personal Notes

ON SUBMIT

An action triggered when a form is submitted.

What Developers Mean:

An event that runs when a form is completed and sent.

Plain English:

When you press the final 'send' button.

Real-Life Example:

Submitting a login form.
Sending a contact message.

How to Say It to AI:

"Run this function on submit of the form."

Personal Notes

PARAMETER

Information passed into a function.

What Developers Mean:

A variable listed in a function definition that receives a value when the function is called.

Plain English:

Instructions you give the machine.

Real-Life Example:

calculateTotal(price, tax)

How to Say It to AI:

"Add two parameters to the function: price and quantity."

Personal Notes

REFRESH

Reloading content or updating the screen.

What Developers Mean:

Re-rendering a component or reloading data to reflect new changes.

Plain English:

Update what's shown.

Real-Life Example:

Pulling down to refresh social media feed.

How to Say It to AI:

"Refresh the page after submission."

Personal Notes

RENDER

Displaying something on the screen.

What Developers Mean:

The process of generating UI elements based on data or state.

Plain English:

Make it appear.

Real-Life Example:

Displaying a list of products.

How to Say It to AI:

"Render the product list dynamically."

Personal Notes

STATE

The current condition of the app.

What Developers Mean:

Stored data that determines how components behave or appear.

Plain English:

The app's current memory.

Real-Life Example:

Cart has 3 items.
User is logged in.
Menu is open.

How to Say It to AI:

"Create state to track whether the modal is open."

Personal Notes

VARIABLE

A named storage space for data.

What Developers Mean:

A container that stores values which can change over time.

Plain English:

A labeled box that holds information.

Real-Life Example:

UserName = "Emma"
CartTotal = 59.99

How to Say It to AI:

"Create a variable to store the user's name."

Personal Notes

SECTION 3

DATA & SYSTEMS

API

A bridge that allows two systems to communicate.

What Developers Mean:

An Application Programming Interface (API) is a defined set of rules that allows software applications to send and receive data from each other.

Plain English:

A messenger that carries information between apps.

Real-Life Example:

Your weather app asks a weather service for today's forecast.
Your payment system connects to Stripe to process a card.

How to Say It to AI:

"Connect this app to an API to retrieve product data."

Personal Notes

AUTHENTICATION

Verifying who someone is before giving access.

What Developers Mean:

A security process that confirms a user's identity through credentials such as passwords, tokens, or biometric data.

Plain English:

Proving you are who you say you are.

Real-Life Example:

Logging in with email and password.
Using Face ID to unlock an app.

How to Say It to AI:

"Add authentication so users must log in before accessing the dashboard."

Personal Notes

BACKEND

The hidden system that runs behind the scenes.

What Developers Mean:

Server-side logic that handles data processing, database communication, authentication, and business rules.

Plain English:

The engine under the hood.

Real-Life Example:

Saving orders.
Storing user accounts.
Calculating totals.

How to Say It to AI:

"Set up a backend to store user profiles securely."

Personal Notes

CLOUD

Internet-based storage and computing.

What Developers Mean:

Remote servers that store data and run applications instead of using a local computer.

Plain English:

Your data living online instead of on your device.

Real-Life Example:

Google Drive.
iCloud backups.

How to Say It to AI:

"Store uploaded files in cloud storage."

Personal Notes

DATABASE

A structured system for storing information.

What Developers Mean:

An organized collection of data that can be queried, updated, and managed efficiently.

Plain English:

A digital filing cabinet.

Real-Life Example:

Customer information.
Product inventory.
Blog posts.

How to Say It to AI:

"Create a database to store user information."

Personal Notes

DOMAIN

The name of your website.

What Developers Mean:

A human-readable web address that maps to a server's IP address.

Plain English:

Your website's street name.

Real-Life Example:

www.yourbrand.com

How to Say It to AI:

"Connect this app to my custom domain."

Personal Notes

ENDPOINT

A specific location within an API.

What Developers Mean:

A URL where an API receives or sends data for a specific function.

Plain English:

A specific door inside a larger building.

Real-Life Example:

/api/products
/api/users

How to Say It to AI:

"Send a request to the products endpoint."

Personal Notes

FRONTEND

The part of the app users see and interact with.

What Developers Mean:

Client-side code that controls layout, design, and user interaction.

Plain English:

Everything visible on the screen.

Real-Life Example:

Buttons, menus, product listings.

How to Say It to AI:

"Build a responsive frontend layout."

Personal Notes

HOSTING

Where your website or app lives online.

What Developers Mean:

A service that provides server space to store and serve your website files.

Plain English:

Renting space on the internet.

Real-Life Example:

Uploading your site so people can access it publicly.

How to Say It to AI:

"Deploy this site to hosting."

Personal Notes

SERVER

A computer that provides data or services to other computers.

What Developers Mean:

A remote system that processes requests and delivers responses over the internet.

Plain English:

The computer that answers requests.

Real-Life Example:

When you open a website, a server sends the page to you.

How to Say It to AI:

"Set up a server to handle API requests."

Personal Notes

SECTION 4

DESIGN & UX

ACCESSIBILITY

Designing products so everyone can use them.

What Developers Mean:

Creating interfaces that are usable by people with disabilities, including visual, auditory, motor, and cognitive impairments.

Plain English:

Making sure no one is left out.

Real-Life Example:

High contrast text.
Screen reader compatibility.
Larger tap targets.

How to Say It to AI:

"Ensure this layout follows accessibility best practices."

Personal Notes

ALIGNMENT

Positioning elements in a clean, structured way.

What Developers Mean:

Arranging elements so they line up consistently along edges or centers.

Plain English:

Making things look organized instead of messy.

Real-Life Example:

Text aligned left.
Buttons centered evenly.

How to Say It to AI:

"Align all elements to the left with consistent spacing."

Personal Notes

MARGIN

Space outside an element.

What Developers Mean:

The external spacing between an element and surrounding elements.

Plain English:

Breathing room around something.

Real-Life Example:

Space between two sections.

How to Say It to AI:

"Add 20px margin between sections."

Personal Notes

PADDING

Space inside an element.

What Developers Mean:

Internal spacing between the content of an element and its border.

Plain English:

Cushioning inside a box.

Real-Life Example:

Space between button text and its edges.

How to Say It to AI:

"Add 16px padding inside the card."

Personal Notes

PROTOTYPE

A preview version of an app or design.

What Developers Mean:

An interactive mockup used to test functionality and user experience before development.

Plain English:

A test drive before building the real thing.

Real-Life Example:

A clickable demo of a new app.

How to Say It to AI:

"Create a simple prototype of this onboarding flow."

Personal Notes

RESPONSIVE

A design that adapts to different screen sizes.

What Developers Mean:

Layouts that automatically adjust using flexible grids and breakpoints.

Plain English:

It rearranges itself so it doesn't look broken.

Real-Life Example:

Website that works on phone and desktop.

How to Say It to AI:

"Make this layout responsive for mobile and tablet."

Personal Notes

TYPOGRAPHY

The style and appearance of text.

What Developers Mean:

The selection and arrangement of fonts, sizes, spacing, and hierarchy to improve readability.

Plain English:

How your text looks and feels.

Real-Life Example:

Large bold headings.
Smaller body text.

How to Say It to AI:

"Use clean, modern typography with strong hierarchy."

Personal Notes

UI (USER INTERFACE)

The visual design of an app or website.

What Developers Mean:

The visual elements users interact with buttons, icons, layout, and styling.

Plain English:

How it looks.

Real-Life Example:

Color scheme, buttons, layout structure..

How to Say It to AI:

"Design a modern UI with neutral colors."

Personal Notes

UX (USER EXPERIENCE)

How users feel when using your product.

What Developers Mean:

The overall experience a user has when interacting with a system, including usability, clarity, and satisfaction.

Plain English:

How easy and enjoyable it is to use.

Real-Life Example:

Clear checkout process.
Simple navigation.

How to Say It to AI:

"Improve the UX by simplifying the checkout steps."

Personal Notes

WIREFRAME

A basic layout sketch of a page.

What Developers Mean:

A low-fidelity visual outline that shows structure without final design details.

Plain English:

The blueprint before decorating.

Real-Life Example:

Black and white layout with boxes for images and text.

How to Say It to AI:

"Create a wireframe for a product page."

Personal Notes

SECTION 5

DEVELOPMENT PROCESS

BUG

An error or flaw in a program.

What Developers Mean:

A defect in code that causes unexpected or incorrect behavior.

Plain English:

Something isn't working the way it should.

Real-Life Example:

Button doesn't respond.
Cart total calculates incorrectly.

How to Say It to AI:

"Run the app to find bug."

Personal Notes

DEBUG

The process of finding and fixing errors.

What Developers Mean:

Systematically identifying and correcting problems in code.

Plain English:

Hunting down what's broken.

Real-Life Example:

Checking console errors.
Testing step-by-step logic.

How to Say It to AI:

"Debug this code and explain what's causing the error."

Personal Notes

DEPLOYMENT

Making your app live and accessible to users.

What Developers Mean:

The process of transferring code from development to a live production environment.

Plain English:

Putting your app online.

Real-Life Example:

Publishing your website so the public can access it.

How to Say It to AI:

"Prepare this project for deployment."

Personal Notes

FRAMEWORK

A structured foundation used to build applications.

What Developers Mean:

A pre-built set of tools and conventions that simplify development.

Plain English:

A construction kit for apps.

Real-Life Example:

React.
Vue.
Django.

How to Say It to AI:

"Build this using a modern JavaScript framework."

Personal Notes

PRODUCTION

The live version of your app used by real users.

What Developers Mean:

The final environment where stable, tested code runs publicly.

Plain English:

The real, public version.

Real-Life Example:

The version customers use daily.

How to Say It to AI:

"Deploy this to production."

Personal Notes

REPOSITORY

A storage location for your project files.

What Developers Mean:

A central location (often online) where code is stored and versioned.

Plain English:

A digital project folder.

Real-Life Example:

A GitHub project.

How to Say It to AI:

"Create a repository for this project."

Personal Notes

TESTING

Checking that everything works correctly.

What Developers Mean:

Running structured tests to confirm functionality and prevent errors.

Plain English:

Making sure it works before going live.

Real-Life Example:

Clicking every button.
Submitting forms with different inputs.

How to Say It to AI:

"Write test cases for this feature."

Personal Notes

UPDATE

Releasing improvements or fixes.

What Developers Mean:

Deploying a new version of software that includes enhancements or patches.

Plain English:

An improved version.

Real-Life Example:

App update in the App Store.

How to Say It to AI:

"Prepare an update that fixes reported bugs."

Personal Notes

VERSION

A specific release of your software.

What Developers Mean:

A labeled iteration of software indicating changes or improvements.

Plain English:

A numbered edition.

Real-Life Example:

Version 1.0
Version 2.1.4

How to Say It to AI:

"Tag this as version 1.0."

Personal Notes

Common Beginner Tech Mistakes

Starting something new in tech can feel overwhelming, especially when everyone seems to "already know" the language.

Here are some of the most common mistakes beginners make and how to avoid them.

1. Confusing Backend and Frontend
   Frontend is what users see.
   Backend is what runs behind the scenes.
   If you mix them up, you'll struggle to describe your project clearly.

2. Giving AI Vague Instructions
   Saying:
   "Build me an app."
   Is too broad.
   Instead say:
   "Build a simple 3-page app with a login screen and a product list."
   Clarity creates better results.

3. Ignoring User Experience (UX)
   Just because something works doesn't mean it's easy to use.
   Good tech isn't just functional, it's intuitive.

4. Copying Code Without Understanding Terms
   Copying and pasting can help you move forward.
   But if you don't understand words like function, state, or API, you'll feel stuck later.
   Vocabulary builds independence.

5. Thinking You're "Bad at Tech"
   You're not.
   You were just handed a language you weren't taught.
   Now you're learning it.

Why These Mistakes Happen

Most beginners don't struggle with logic.

They struggle with terminology.

When you don't understand the words, everything feels more complicated than it actually is.

Tech isn't magic.

It's structured language.

Once you understand:

- What the pieces are called
- How they connect
- What each term really means

You move from confusion to clarity.
That's the purpose of this book.

Before You Start Your First Tech Project

Use this checklist before building an app, website or AI workflow.

Clarity Check

- ☐ Can I explain my idea in one simple sentence?
- ☐ Do I understand the key terms involved?
- ☐ Do I know what problem this solves?

Structure Check

- ☐ Do I know what the frontend will include?
- ☐ Do I know what the backend needs to store?
- ☐ Do I need an API connection?

AI Prompt Check

- ☐ Am I being specific in my instructions?
- ☐ Have I clearly stated constraints and goals?
- ☐ Did I ask AI to explain anything unclear?

Clarity saves time.
Specificity saves money.

The Difference Is Vocabulary

The gap between confusion and confidence isn't intelligence.
It's language.

When you don't understand the words, tech feels overwhelming.
When you understand the words, the system becomes logical.

Backend.
Frontend.
API.
State.
Deployment.

They aren't mysterious anymore.
They're tools.
And tools are meant to be used.

You don't need to know everything.
You just need to know what things are called and what they do.

That's how conversations become clearer.
That's how AI gives better results.
That's how ideas become real projects.

Tech Words for Normal Humans.

Now the words are yours.

You're More Ready Than You Think.

If this book helped you, please consider leaving a review.
Your feedback helps other beginners find clarity too.

Made in the USA
Monee, IL
11 November 2026

fa52fadd-1beb-4e6a-b25c-1c0ef26abd37R01